Thank you!

By Janine Amos

Illustrated by Annabel Spenceley

CHERRYTREE BOOKS

A Cherrytree Book

Designed and produced
by A S Publishing

First published in 1998
by Cherrytree Books
a division of the Evans Publishing Group
2A Portman Mansions
Chiltern St
London W1U 6NR

Reprinted 2002 (twice), 2004

British Library Cataloguing in Publication Data

Amos, Janine
    Thank you!. – (Good manners)
    1.Interpersonal relations – Juvenile literature
    I.Title II.Spenceley, Annabel
    395.1'22

ISBN 1 84234 125 1

Printed in Malaysia

Sam's birthday

It's Sam's birthday.

His friends come to play.

Sam's gran gives him a present.
Sam forgets to say Thank you.

He goes on playing.
How does Gran feel?

Sam opens his present.
He remembers to say Thank you!

He gives Gran a hug.

How does Gran feel now?

Billy's
spaceship

Billy's building a spaceship.
It's hard work.

Joe gives him a hand.
They build it together.

13

The spaceship is finished.

Billy forgets to say Thank you.

How do you think Joe feels?

Billy shows his dad.

Billy remembers Joe.

Billy thanks Joe.

How does Joe feel now?

Kelly's mum

Everyone is playing at Kelly's.
Kelly's mum gives them juice.

Kelly's mum makes them a snack.

Kelly's mum helps them dress up.

It's time to go home.
How is Kelly's mum feeling?

25

Kelly thinks about it.

Kelly thanks her mum.

The other children thank her too.

How is Kelly's mum feeling now?

"*People like to feel valued.*
If someone gives you something – their help,
their time or a present – don't forget to say
Thank you."